Dear Family and Friends of New Readers,

Welcome to Scholastic Reader. We have taken more than eighty years of experience with teachers, parents, and children and put it into a program that is designed to match your child's interest and skills. Each Scholastic Reader is designed to support your child's efforts to learn how to read at every age and every stage.

- First Reader
- Preschool - Kindergarten
- ABC's
- First words

- Beginning Reader
- Preschool - Grade 1
- Sight words
- Words to sound out
- Simple sentences

- Developing Reader
- Grades 1 – 2
- New vocabulary
- Longer sentences

- Growing Reader
- Grades 1 – 3
- Reading for inspiration and information

On the back of every book, we have indicated the grade level, guided reading level, Lexile® level, and word count. You can use this information to find a book that is a good fit for your child.

For ideas about sharing books with your new reader, please visit www.scholastic.com. Enjoy helping your child learn to read and love to read!

Happy Reading!

—Francie Alexander
Chief Academic Officer
Scholastic Inc.

ISBN-13: 978-0-545-07233-5
ISBN-10: 0-545-07233-6

12 11 10 9 8   12 13 14/0

Printed in the U.S.A.   40
First printing, May 2009

GROWING READER

LEVEL **3**

700-1500 WORDS

OCEAN GIANTS

KATE WATERS

SCHOLASTIC INC.

New York   Toronto   London   Auckland   Sydney
Mexico City   New Delhi   Hong Kong   Buenos Aires

The ocean is home to many
amazing creatures. Sharks, seals,
whales, and walruses live there. Other
creatures, such as the giant clam and
the huge green moray eel, do too.

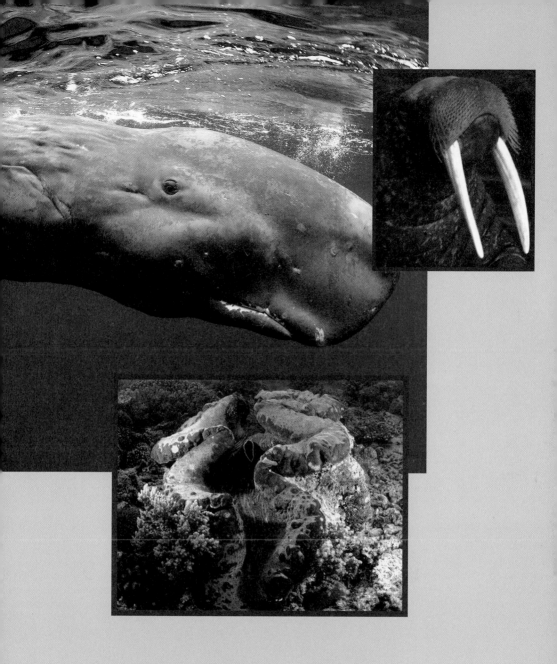

This book will introduce you to weird and wonderful animals. Some are shy. Others attack. All are ocean giants.

Some animals live near the surface of the ocean. Some live in the middle. Others live close to the bottom.

Many animals swim between layers. They dive to catch food and swim to the surface to breathe. Others animals live in the ocean and on land.

The ocean covers more than seventy percent of Earth's surface.

This adult female blue whale is next to a research boat that is 23 feet long.

The largest living animal is the blue whale. This whale can be 100 feet long. Blue whales have baleen instead of teeth. The baleen is a set of strong, thin plates. They are made of the same material as your fingernails.

This southern right whale is sifting water through its baleen.

Almost 400 baleen plates hang down from the blue whale's upper jaw. The baleen works like a filter. It strains water out. Then the whale eats the tiny animals that remain.

The largest whale with teeth is the sperm whale. Sperm whales are about 60 feet long. They can weigh as much as an airplane. They have large, high foreheads and big brains.

Sperm whales dive deep into the ocean to find food. They can spend more than one hour underwater hunting squid and large fish. Then they have to come to the surface to breathe through their blowholes.

The beautiful orca, or killer whale, is not a whale at all. It is the largest of the dolphins. Orcas can weigh 12,000 pounds. They live in groups called pods. An orca stays with its pod for its whole life.

Orcas are very vocal. They click, whistle, and scream. They are curious and sometimes swim close to boats. Orcas also leap out of the water. This is called breaching.

The great white shark is the giant of the shark world. Great whites can be 17 to 36 feet long. They eat fish and other sea animals. They will also eat humans.

Great whites swim with their mouths open. They have between 5 and 15 rows of teeth. A back tooth moves forward when the tooth in front of it falls out. Each tooth has a jagged edge. This helps the shark tear up its food.

Walruses and seals live in the water and on land. Walruses are excellent swimmers. They can be 12 feet tall and weigh as much as 3,000 pounds. Walruses use their long tusks to dig on the ocean floor for clams and other shellfish.

The largest seal is the elephant seal. It gets its name from its floppy nose. Elephant seals are champion divers. They can dive down 4,000 feet.

Manatees are gentle giants. They have no natural enemies. They live in warm water near the coast and munch on sea grasses. Manatees move their tails to swim. They only use their flippers to steer and to pull themselves close to the plants they eat.

Manatees move slowly. Signs warn boaters to watch out for manatees.

MANATEE ZONE
SLOW SPEED
MINIMUM WAKE

Giant squid capturing an octopus.

Giant squid have 5 pairs of arms,
or tentacles. Each arm is 30 feet long.
Squid move by squirting out jets of
water. They squirt dark ink when they
want to hide or when they are upset.
Giant squid have the largest eyes of
any animal.

In 2007 a fishing boat in New Zealand captured a new kind of squid. It is called the colossal squid because scientists think it might be even bigger than this giant squid!

The giant clam is strong. It can break a diver's leg when its shell snaps shut. Its shell can weigh 400 pounds. Giant clams live in coral reefs in the South Pacific and Indian Oceans.

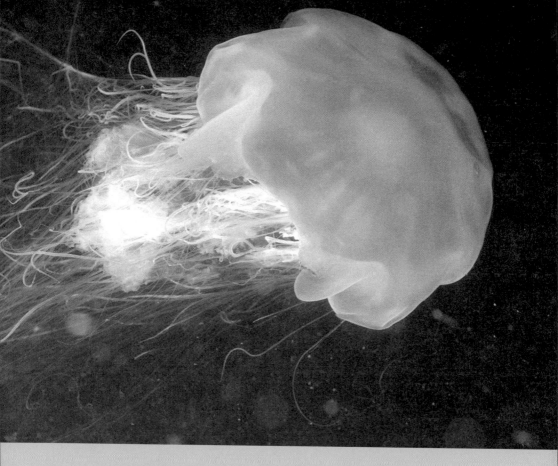

The biggest jellyfish is the Arctic lion's mane jellyfish. Its trailing tentacles can be 100 feet long. This jellyfish lives deep in the ocean near the North Pole. It captures small fish and other creatures in its poisonous tentacles.

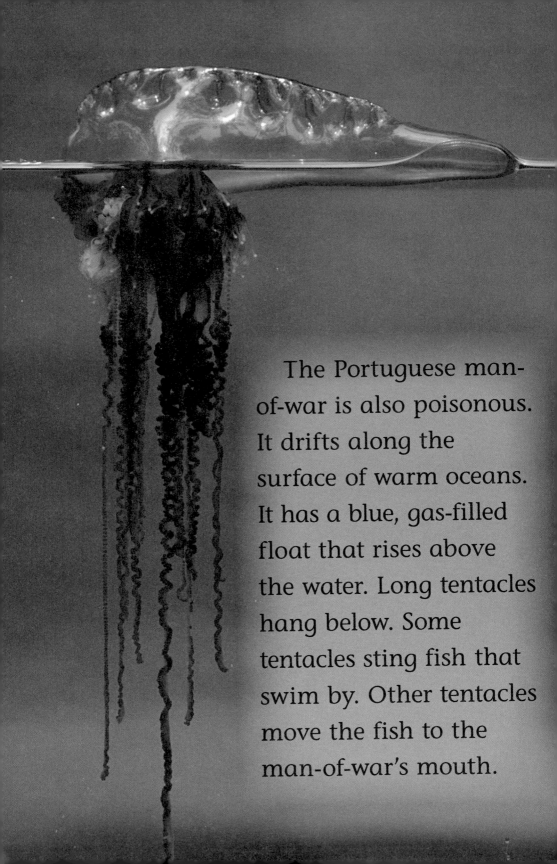

The Portuguese man-of-war is also poisonous. It drifts along the surface of warm oceans. It has a blue, gas-filled float that rises above the water. Long tentacles hang below. Some tentacles sting fish that swim by. Other tentacles move the fish to the man-of-war's mouth.

The Giant Pacific octopus is very shy. It hides from divers. Its arms can spread 12 feet across. It catches fish and other food with the suckers on its arms. The Giant Pacific octopus can change colors to blend into its surroundings.

Manta rays are the biggest rays. Their diamond-shaped bodies make them fast swimmers. The largest manta ray can weigh 3,000 pounds. It can grow to be 23 feet across. Mantas are very curious. They will swim near divers and boats.

This scuba diver is swimming safely under a manta ray.

The green moray eel is very, very dangerous. It can be five to ten feet long. It has very powerful jaws. This eel hides in coral reefs. It darts out to catch its prey with its sharp teeth.

All ocean creatures need food and clean water to survive. But many ocean giants are in danger. Some people think that we fish too much. That means there are fewer fish for ocean animals to eat. We also pollute the ocean by dumping huge amounts of waste into it. And some people hunt ocean animals. Some of these animals are close to extinction. Many people are working to pass laws to protect the ocean habitat.

A sea lion caught in a fishing net

Scientists have not discovered all of the animals that live in the ocean. There are still places to explore and new creatures to find. Ocean explorers travel to the deepest parts of the ocean. Who knows what new ocean giants they will discover?

The Mir 1 *submersible observes sea life.*

Glossary

blowhole—the hole on the top of a whale's head that it breathes through

breach—to break through something. A whale breaches by breaking through the surface of the water.

coral—a substance made up of the skeletons of tiny sea creatures

coral reef—a strip of coral near the edge of the ocean that has hardened into rock

jagged—uneven and sharp

pod—a group of animals that live and travel together

shellfish—a sea creature with a shell, such as a shrimp, crab, lobster, or mussel

tentacle—one of the long arms of some animals, such as octopus and squid. Tentacles are used for moving, feeling, and grasping.

tusk—the long, curved, pointed tooth of a walrus, elephant, wild boar, and other animals